Choose a topic and start to practise writing. Each booklet has a theme to help you start to write…stories, reports, articles, letters and many more. Start collecting them now.

Guinea Pig creative writing booklets also provide extra practice for children who have completed:

- Creative Story Writing ISBN: 9780955831508
- Persuasive Writing & Argument ISBN: 9780955831515
- Information Writing ISBN: 9780955831522

They are for:

* children who are working at Key Stage 2 of the National Curriculum, levels 3-5 (in Years 5 and 6 of primary school),
* children who are working at Key Stage 3, levels 3-5 (Years 7 and 8 of Secondary School).

They provide practice for all 9-13 year olds, especially children taking 11+ examinations.

© **Copyright 2011**

Written by Sally A Jones and Amanda C Jones

Published by GUINEA PIG EDUCATION

2 Cobs Way,
New Haw,
Addlestone,
Surrey,
KT15 3AF.

www.guineapigeducation.co.uk

Let's **learn** to *write* <u>fiction</u>.

When you *write fiction*, <u>**you must**</u>:

1. Decide who will be your audience?

2. Think of different genres – realistic, detective, ghost, gothic horror.

3. Ask what is the purpose of my writing?

When you *write to entertain*, remember that <u>**you must**</u> :

1. Have an interesting opening and a memorable ending

2. Have good characters, setting and plot

3. Build up suspense

4. Use dialogue – to move the story along

5. Use a variety of simple, compound and complex sentences

Plan your fiction writing:

<table>
<tr><td>

PARAGRAPH 1

- Start with a memorable first sentence to make the reader want to read on.

- Introduce the characters and the setting.

- Introduce the plot.

</td><td>

Write:

- in **FIRST PERSON**, so you are the main character telling the story (using I or we).

or

- in **THIRD PERSON** (using he or she) as if you were a fly watching from the wall.

</td></tr>
<tr><td>

PARAGRAPH 2

- Develop the plot.

- What might happen to trigger off a series of events?

- Build up suspense.

</td><td rowspan="2">

Remember:

- Use connectives or conjunctions:

- *and or but (to join compound sentences)*
- *or, so, if, when, while, after, before, because, unless, until, whereas, although (to join complex sentences)*
- *use pronouns - who, which, whose, what, that*
- *to link ideas use - firstly, later, therefore, on the other hand, at that moment, by this time, next, soon...*

- Use a range of sentences – simple, compound and complex sentences

- Use 'we' to identify with the reader.

- Use 'you' for second person - in persuasive pieces and to speak directly to the reader.

</td></tr>
<tr><td>

PARAGRAPH 3

- Wind up your story with a good ending. In the resolution you will have solved all the problems.

- It could be happy, sad, a cliff hanger (which leaves the reader to make up his or her own mind), or a moral ending

- Have a memorable final sentence.

</td></tr>
</table>

<u>The Art Gallery</u>

Every year, the city gallery held an art exhibition, but I only remember one of them because it still haunts me. The exhibition presented a collection of famous paintings, old masters by painters who lived over four hundred years ago. I was dragged round it by Uncle Jim and my sister Kath because they were both crazy about art. I pretended to be interested in those old paintings, (though history was my least favourite subject). Can you imagine the scene in the gallery? There were crowds of people, walking round as slow as snails, taking ten minutes to study each painting. I was staring reluctantly at some old canvases, which portrayed strange people in weird, old-fashioned costumes. They were sitting in rooms as dark as pitch, full of antique furnishings. Through the windows of their houses, I saw a landscape stretching into nothingness, which consisted of green trees, rolling hills and a grey lake. Seriously, how could they lead a happy life in those places: with no technology, no cars, planes or computers? That's why I stared blankly at each canvas, pretending to be interested, but thinking about the burger and chips they served in the restaurant.

I jumped the queue of art connoisseurs and wandered off on my own. Uncle Jim and Kathryn were being annoying, ambling round so slowly, commenting on every little detail in each painting. I wanted to move quickly, so I could get to the café. Anyway, what harm could come to me in here? I left the main hall and entered a small side room. Immediately, I sensed it had a mysterious atmosphere; it was strangely empty. There was only one painting on the end wall. The artist had painted a scene of a rich family, (a duke and duchess and their kids perhaps), eating a lavish feast. The food was set out on a huge table, lit by a giant candelabrum. The flickering flames of the candles lit up the pale, sad faces of the people at the table. It lit the faces of the musicians who were entertaining them. One man was dressed in a clown's costume. Satisfied, that I had learnt enough about the life of these people, I turned to go.

At that moment, I heard a low voice. It was
hardly audible, but it was calling my name.
"Come closer Stephen", it croaked like a
toad. "I want to have a word with you." I
turned round, expecting to see the curator,
but to my surprise there was no one there.
Was the voice coming from the painting?
NO of course not! I dismissed this crazy
thought instantly, until I caught the eye of the
ominous looking clown in the painting. He
fixed his gaze on me. His mouth twitched.
His thin bony finger beckoned me to come
closer. In a mad moment, I went over to him
and stared up into those sad, black eyes.

"I have a proposition to make to you boy. Yes, you down there." I stared dumbfounded. "Why
don't we swap places, you and me? You can come into my seventeenth century world and wear
this ridiculous costume and I'll be a modern boy." I stood speechless trying to grasp what was
happening. Before I could reply, to my absolute horror, he started to move slowly, very slowly
from his position, "No, no, no, I stammered…the modern world is stressful, there's pollution... our
technology breaks down... You'd need loads of money." But, he was clambering down from the
painting, reaching out for my arm to help him down. Suddenly, the movement caused the painting
to tip. Then it crashed down. BANG! It fell on the floor. It smashed in several pieces. My head was
spinning and I was falling, falling…

Alerted by the security alarm (that goes off automatically if a valuable painting is touched), the
curator strolled briskly into the room,
"What's going on he demanded to know? That painting is priceless. How did it fall? I'll call the
police…"
"It just fell off the wall," insisted a man with a soft croaky voice, "and I think it may have bumped
this young man." I found myself sitting on the floor, dazed from a bump on my head. Uncle Jim
and Kath were fussing over me; someone was applying first aid, "Are you sure you're all right?"
asked the soft voiced man, staring down at me with a weird expression. Was that a twinkle in his
eye? He bore an uncanny resemblance to somebody familiar, but after the bump on my head I felt
confused. "Who is he," I pondered? I watched him leave by the exit and he went out into the real
world. .

A week later, I went back to the city gallery. In all that confusion at the art gallery, I'd mislaid both
my jacket and rucksack. Had they turned up in lost property? No! There was definitely nothing of
mine there. Browsing through the items, I couldn't help be a little surprised at the kind of things
people lose. Who would lose a strange fancy dress costume, a clown outfit for example? The
mind boggles. By this time, the painting had been completely restored, with no signs of any
damage. It had been re-hung and out of curiosity I went to look at it. It seemed totally different, I
thought. It was fresher, less sinister. The people looked happier. Was one of the figures missing?
It was all coming back to me now. Oh no! It couldn't be… Could it?

Don't forget to **<u>STRUCTURE</u>** your story.

It means organise your story so it has a beginning, middle and end.

Find out more about structuring a story.

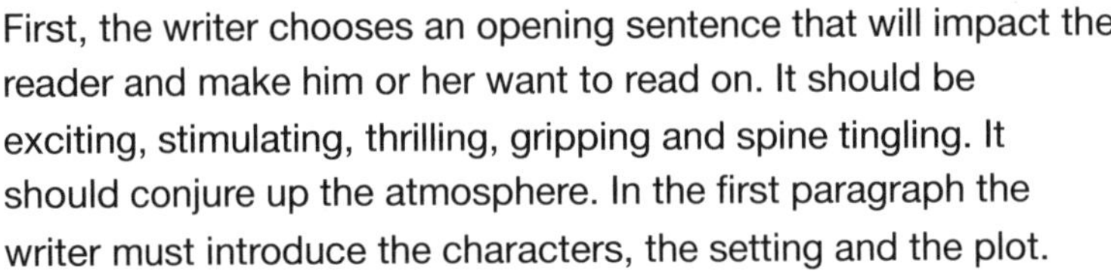

First, the writer chooses an opening sentence that will impact the reader and make him or her want to read on. It should be exciting, stimulating, thrilling, gripping and spine tingling. It should conjure up the atmosphere. In the first paragraph the writer must introduce the characters, the setting and the plot.

Alternatively, the writer could:

- start straight into the action

- introduce the characters and plot using dialogue.

- start by describing the setting.

Now develop the plot of the story. Are things going well in your story? Introduce a complication in the story line – a problem – a mystery – something the characters have to overcome. Move the events on at a fast pace. If there is lots of action, it will be exciting for your reader, so he or she is eager to see what happens next.

Keep building up suspense in your story. Towards the end of the second paragraph, your main character is in some danger. He or she is in a difficult situation. What will happen? Will he survive? Use short statements. Use ! or ? or words like 'suddenly'. Your reader must be gripped by fear – suspense – excitement – doubt or anger. This is the climax. Your reader will want to know how the story will end.

You must have a good ending or resolution. In the last paragraph, you must wind up events with a satisfactory conclusion.

- It might be a happy ending – where characters live happily ever after.

- A surprise cliffhanger ending - where the reader has to draw his or her own conclusion about what really happens.

- It might be a sad ending or a moral ending – with a comment from the author, 'It taught me never to go off on my own again.'

Whatever ending you decide on, make the last line memorable for your reader.

Now write the story you planned.

A Strange Meeting

Uncle Jim was fanatical about old paintings and he was driving me crazy. He was always asking me if I knew the work of this or that famous artist. What's more, he would travel miles to visit galleries. One morning, he rung my mum and asked if I could go with him to Paris. It was school holidays (and I had nothing else to do), so I reluctantly said I would go. He assured mum it would be the experience of a lifetime. I thought, "he doesn't really know me, I don't know the right end of a paintbrush. I don't ever paint myself and I don't need to look at other peoples' work, especially when they're 150 years old."

A few days later, we were sight seeing in Paris. We had a quick look at all the famous landmarks. We'd been up the Eiffel Tower (at least to the first stage). We'd seen the Arc de Triomphe and taken a motorboat up the Seine. Things were going surprisingly well. Then, my uncle announced, "Now, we're going to the art gallery." Before I knew it, we were in a vast hall. It was cold, it was still, and it was echoey. You know the kind of place. Where they say, 'Don't go near that... don't touch that... don't even breathe'. Anyway, Uncle Jim just stood in front of one of his favourite paintings for hours so I wandered off.

In the next room, the paintings were quite different. They were more modern. When I peered at them closely, it looked like the painter had gone crazy with a brush and just put blobs or dabs of paint all over the place. Intrigued, I just stepped up to look at one of the paintings closer. A weird sensation came over me. My legs were as wobbly as a jelly. I WAS GOING IN!....................................
Yes, I wasn't in the marble hall anymore. I was somewhere else! Where was I?
"HELP!" I cried...

● Now write your own ending to the story.

- Has the boy or girl gone inside a painting?
- Which painting?
- Who was it by?
- Where does he or she go?
- What happens next?
- How is the situation resolved?

Your Ending

....
....
....
....
....
....
....
....
....
....
....
....
....
....
....
....
....
....
....
....
....

Now read the suggested ending below.

You will have guessed, I had been transported to some far away place. Everywhere looked strange. Was I in a different time zone? I was out in the fresh air, on a boat on the river. It was early morning. A bright red sun was rising over the water. The sun was a ball of fire (metaphor), blazing in the water. Its reflection filled the shimmering ripples with many colours. Who was this man who sat beside me in the boat? He was a stout gentleman wearing an old fashioned straw hat and he was beckoning me over.

"May I introduce myself," he beamed. "Monet, Claud Monet, artist."

"Tom," I replied reticently.

"I'm delighted to meet you young man," he exclaimed. "Nothing wrong, I hope, you look upset. It's a lovely morning," he added softly in a French accent, "so I've captured this beautiful sunrise in my painting. Help me put in the last few strokes."

"I don't paint," I replied, "I'd mess it up."

"No, no," I insist, "have a go. Just brush the paint on in little strokes. It's easy," he insisted, pressing another paint brush into my hand. Together, we splashed on colours for what seemed like hours and hours.

"You'll make a great artist some day," he assured me.

At that moment, the man's voice began to drift away on the wind until I couldn't hear it any longer. When I looked up, it was not Monet but Uncle Jim who stood beside me. We were both looking at the same painting. I bet you don't know who painted this do you?

""Impressionism, 'Sunset' by Claude Monet, he is one of my favourite artists, it is a work of genius, don't you think?" I said, wide eyed. He stared back at me in amazement.

"In fact uncle, Monet has convinced me... He's convinced me to study art. From now on I'm going to be an artist." Uncle smiled disbelievingly. I was driving him crazy.

FACTS about the *artist* Claude Monet.

CHILDHOOD

- Monet was born on 14h November 1840.
- From the age of 5, he was brought up in Le Havre in Northern France.
- He enjoyed watching the fishermen at the port.
- At school he drew boats.
- At 8 years old, Monet sold his first painting.
- The proprietor of a painting shop let him display his paintings in the window.
- People pressed their noses up to the window to see his amazing work.

YOUNG PERSON

- A famous painter invited Monet to join him on a painting weekend on the beach.
- After this experience, Monet decided to become a painter.
- His parents were horrified.
- They wanted their son to take up a respectable profession.
- At 20 years old, Monet enrolled in a school of art.
- His aunt gave him some money.
- She loved painting and believed in the talent of her nephew.
- She was convinced Monet would become a great painter one day.

EARLY PAINTING

- Monet liked to work in the country with his painter friends.
- Not far from Paris, in the forests of Fontainebleau, he would set up his easel and paint the countryside and the people who were walking at the weekend.
- He especially liked to paint the sun reflecting on the water.
- He gave birth to a new style.
- He used little blobs and dabs of colour on his brush to form impressions.
- Nothing was realistic.

FAMILY LIFE

- Monet married wife Camille.
- At this time, he painted scenes of his family. His wife and children often appear in his paintings.
- He sold his paintings for small amounts of money, so his family were quite poor, but sometimes he was given some commissions to paint.
- His fellow painter Renoir also helped him with money.

- The first impressionist art exhibition took place in 1874 in Paris.
- Monet exhibited a painting called Impression of a Sun Rise.
- After having seen this painting, an art critic started to call his work impressionism.

IMPRESSIONISM

- The impressionist artists included: Monet, Renoir, Pissarro and Sisley
- They used to paint outside.
- They tried to paint light. Monet used several canvases at the same time to try to capture the moment when the light changes, so he painted the sea in blue, green and white. He used eighteen canvases in the same day, as he painted Rouen Cathedral, blue in the morning, pale yellow at noon and pink in the evening.
- They painted outside, so they could paint the colours of nature. The painted water so it sparkled, leaves to reflect the sun and even stone walls could shimmer.
- Impressionist artists painted everyday life and the new technology of the day, like steam trains.
- They used three primary colours: red, blue and yellow and mixed them into other colours but never used black.
- At first, people did not understand the paintings because they were not realistic like photos.

LATER LIFE

- Other famous painting by Monet include: paintings of the seaside, of lakes, Rouen Cathedral, of London, water lilies, the Japanese bridge and the haystack.
- After Camille's death, at the age of 32, he married family friend Alice in 1883.
- Monet bought a boat which he turned into an art studio.
- By the time he was forty, impressionism had become popular and Monet had achieved success. His paintings sold in the United States and Paris.
- In old age, when he was painting the water lilies, he nearly went blind and had to have an operation on his eyes.
- He died in Giverney at the age of 86.

Write an information leaflet about Monet. Write up these facts about the artist Claude Monet in your own words. Use a variety of sentences: simple, compound and complex. Use good words. First write the introduction. Then, write a series of paragraphs about different aspects of Monet's life. Next, write a conclusion. You could include your opinion about Monet's paintings

Write your information leaflet here.

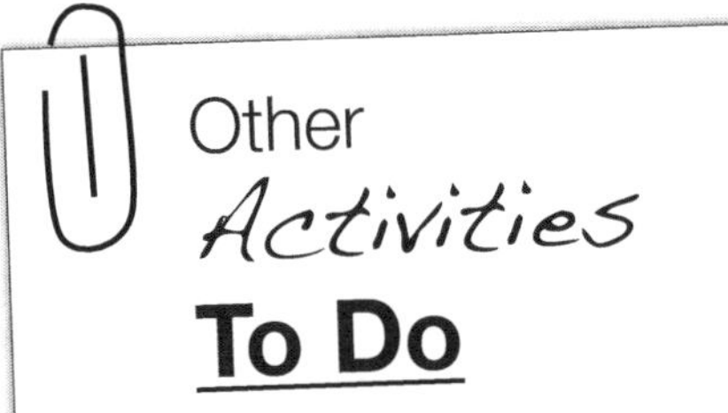

Write a non-fiction leaflet for children about another painter.

Make a list of famous artists (both old and modern). Can you name any of the masterpieces they painted? Use the internet or an encyclopaedia to help you.

For example:

Rembrandt, Constable, Van Gogh, Leonardo Da Vinci, Picasso, Turner

If you could meet an artist like Picasso, one of the most famous painters who ever lived, what would you ask him?

<u>For example:</u>

- Did you paint as a child?
- How did you start painting?
- Where did you learn to paint?
- What do you like to paint?
- ....
- ....
- ....

Think of some more.

Write a humorous dialogue between a mother and a boy or girl who doesn't understand modern art, as they walk round an exhibition. Try drawing a cartoon strip and putting the dialogue in speech bubbles.

<u>For example:</u>

Child	What's that?
Mother	It is a very famous painting. It's a work of art.
Child	It looks like squiggles and strange shapes. It looks like a baby's scribble.
Mother	This type of art is known as modern abstract art.
Child	What is it meant to be a picture of?
	If you look carefully, you can see the artist has painted...

Carry on the dialogue...

Your dialogue:

Made in the USA
Monee, IL
07 July 2026

56544277R00015